Impressum
Verlag: BABADADA GmbH, Nedderfeld 112 , 22529 Hamburg
Geschäftsführer / Verlagsleitung: Harald Hof
Druck: Books on Demand GmbH, In de Tarpen 42, 22848 Norderstedt

Imprint
Publisher: BABADADA GmbH, Nedderfeld 112 , 22529 Hamburg, Germany
Managing Director / Publishing direction: Harald Hof
Print: Books on Demand GmbH, In de Tarpen 42, 22848 Norderstedt

Schule
school

Klassenzimmer
classroom

dividieren
divide

186/2

Tafel
board

Schulhof
school yard

Lehrer
teacher

Papier
paper

schreiben
write

Stift
pen

Schreibtisch
desk

Lineal
ruler

Buch
book

Schüler
pupil

Schultasche

satchel

Federmappe

pencil case

Bleistift

pencil

Bleistiftspitzer

pencil sharpener

Radierer

rubber

Zeichenblock

drawing pad

Zeichnung

drawing

Pinsel

paintbrush

Malkasten

paint box

Schere

scissors

Klebstoff

glue

Übungsheft

exercise book

Hausübung

homework

Zahl

number

addieren

add

subtrahieren

subtract

multiplizieren

multiply

rechnen

calculate

Buchstabe

letter

Alphabet

alphabet

Wort

word

Text

text

lesen

read

Kreide

chalk

Unterrichtsstunde

lesson

Klassenbuch

register

Prüfung

exam

Zeugnis

certificate

Schuluniform

school uniform

Ausbildung

education

Lexikon

encyclopedia

Universität

university

Mikroskop

microscope

Karte

map

Papierkorb

waste-paper basket

Hotel
hotel

Herberge
hostel

Wechselstube
bureau de change

Koffer
suitcase

Auto
car

Sprache

language

ja / nein

yes / no

Okay

Okay

Hallo

hello

Dolmetscherin

translator

Danke

Thank you

Wie viel kostet …?

how much is…?

Ich verstehe nicht.

I do not understand

Problem

problem

Guten Abend!

Good evening!

Guten Morgen!

Good morning!

Gute Nacht!

Good night!

Auf Wiederschaun!

bye bye

Richtung

direction

Gepäck

luggage

Tasche

bag

Rucksack

backpack

Gast

guest

Zimmer

room

Schlafsack

sleeping bag

Zelt

tent

Touristeninformation

tourist information

Strand

beach

Kreditkarte

credit card

Frühstück

breakfast

Mittagessen

lunch

Abendessen

dinner

Fahrkarte

ticket

Lift

lift

Briefmarke

stamp

Grenze

border

Zoll

customs

Botschaft

embassy

Visum

visa

Pass

passport

Transport
transport

Flugzeug
aeroplane

Schiff
ship

Feuerwehrauto
fire engine

Bus
bus

Lastwagen
truck

Motorboot
motorboat

Fahrrad
bike

Auto
car

Fähre

ferry

Boot

boat

Motorrad

motorbike

Polizeiauto

police car

Rennauto

racing car

Mietwagen

rental car

Carsharing

car sharing

Abschleppwagen

breakdown truck

Müllwagen

refuse truck

Motor

motor

Kraftstoff

fuel

Tankstelle

petrol station

Verkehrsschild

traffic sign

Verkehr

traffic

Stau

traffic jam

Parkplatz

car park

Bahnhof

train station

Schienen

tracks

Zug

train

Straßenbahn

tram

Wagon

carriage

Transport - transport

Hubschrauber

helicopter

Flughafen

airport

Tower

tower

Passagier

passenger

Container

container

Karton

carton

Rollwagen

cart

Korb

basket

starten / landen

take off / land

Stadt
city

Dorf

village

Stadtzentrum

city centre

Haus

house

Kino
cinema

Werbung
advert

Straßenlaterne
street lamp

Straße
street

Taxi
taxi

Kiosk
snack shop

Fußgänger
pedestrian

Gehsteig
pavement

Zebrastreifen
zebra crossing

Mülltonne
bin

Kreuzung
crossing

Ampel
traffic lights

Hütte

hut

Wohnung

flat

Bahnhof

train station

Rathaus

town hall

Museum

museum

Schule

school

Stadt - city

Universität

university

Bank

bank

Spital

hospital

Hotel

hotel

Apotheke

pharmacy

Büro

office

Buchhandlung

book shop

Geschäft

shop

Blumenladen

florist's

Supermarkt

supermarket

Markt

market

Kaufhaus

department store

Fischhändler

fishmonger's

Einkaufszentrum

shopping centre

Hafen

harbour

Park

park

Bank

bench

Brücke

bridge

Stiege

stairs

U-Bahn

underground

Tunnel

tunnel

Bushaltestelle

bus stop

Bar

bar

Restaurant

restaurant

Briefkasten

postbox

Straßenschild

street sign

Parkuhr

parking meter

Zoo

zoo

Badeanstalt

swimming pool

Moschee

mosque

Bauernhof

farm

Umweltverschmutzung

pollution

Friedhof

graveyard

Kirche

church

Spielplatz

playground

Tempel

temple

Landschaft

landscape

Blatt
leaf

Wegweiser
signpost

Weg
way

Wiese
meadow

Stein
stone

Wanderer
hiker

Baum
tree

Fluss
river

Gras
grass

Blume
flower

Tal

valley

Hügel

hill

See

lake

Wald

forest

Wüste

desert

Vulkan

volcano

Schloss

castle

Regenbogen

rainbow

Pilz

mushroom

Palme

palm tree

Moskito

mosquito

Fliege

fly

Ameise

ant

Biene

bee

Spinne

spider

Käfer

beetle

Frosch

frog

Eichhörnchen

squirrel

Igel

hedgehog

Hase

hare

Eule

owl

Vogel

bird

Schwan

swan

Wildschwein

boar

Hirsch

deer

Elch

moose

Staudamm

dam

Windrad

wind turbine

Solarmodul

solar panel

Klima

climate

Kellner
waiter

Speisekarte
menu

Sessel
chair

Suppe
soup

Pizza
pizza

Besteck
cutlery

Tischdecke
tablecloth

Vorspeise

starter

Hauptgericht

main course

Nachspeise

dessert

Getränke

drinks

Essen

food

Flasche

bottle

Fastfood

fast food

Streetfood

street food

Teekanne

teapot

Zuckerdose

sugar bowl

Portion

portion

Espressomaschine

espresso machine

Kinderstuhl

high chair

Rechnung

bill

Tablett

tray

Messer

knife

Gabel

fork

Löffel

spoon

Teelöffel

teaspoon

Serviette

serviette

Glas

glass

Teller

plate

Suppenteller

soup plate

Untertasse

saucer

Sauce

sauce

Salzstreuer

salt pot

Pfeffermühle

pepper mill

Essig

vinegar

Öl

oil

Gewürze

spices

Ketchup

ketchup

Senf

mustard

Mayonnaise

mayonnaise

Supermarkt
supermarket

Angebot
special offer

Kunde
customer

Milchprodukte
dairy

Obst
fruit

Einkaufswagen
trolley

Schlachterei

butcher's

Bäckerei

baker's

wiegen

weigh

Gemüse

vegetables

Fleisch

meat

Tiefkühlkost

frozen food

Aufschnitt

cold meat

Konserven

tinned food

Waschmittel

washing powder

Süßigkeiten

sweets

Haushaltsartikel

household products

Reinigungsmittel

cleaning products

Verkäuferin

salesperson

Kassa

till

Kassiererin

cashier

Einkaufsliste

shopping list

Öffnungszeiten

opening hours

Brieftasche

wallet

Kreditkarte

credit card

Tasche

bag

Plastiktüte

plastic bag

Wasser

water

Saft

juice

Milch

milk

Cola

coke

Wein

wine

Bier

beer

Alkohol

alcohol

Kakao

cocoa

Tee

tea

Kaffee

coffee

Espresso

espresso

Cappuccino

cappuccino

Banane

banana

Apfel

apple

Orange

orange

Melone

melon

Zitrone

lemon

Karotte

carrot

Knoblauch

garlic

Bambus

bamboo

Zwiebel

onion

Pilz

mushroom

Nüsse

nuts

Nudeln

noodles

Spaghetti

spaghetti

Reis

rice

Salat

salad

Pommes frites

chips

Bratkartoffeln

fried potatoes

Pizza

pizza

Hamburger

hamburger

Sandwich

sandwich

Schnitzel

cutlet

Schinken

ham

Salami

salami

Wurst

sausage

Huhn

chicken

Braten

roast

Fisch

fish

Haferflocken

porridge oats

Müsli

muesli

Cornflakes

cornflakes

Mehl

flour

Croissant

croissant

Semmel

bread roll

Brot

bread

Toast

toast

Kekse

biscuits

Butter

butter

Topfen

curd

Kuchen

cake

Ei

egg

Spiegelei

fried egg

Käse

cheese

Eiscreme

ice cream

Zucker

sugar

Honig

honey

Marmelade

jam

Schokoladenaufstrich

chocolate spread

Curry

curry

Bauernhaus
farmhouse

Strohballen
straw bale

Scheune
barn

Feld
field

Pferd
horse

Anhänger
trailer

Fohlen
foal

Traktor
tractor

Esel
donkey

Schaf
sheep

Lamm
lamb

Ziege

goat

Kuh

cow

Kalb

calf

Schwein

pig

Ferkel

piglet

Stier

bull

Gans

goose

Ente

duck

Küken

chick

Huhn

hen

Hahn

cock

Ratte

rat

Katze

cat

Maus

mouse

Ochse

ox

Hund

dog

Hundehütte

doghouse

Gartenschlauch

garden hose

Gießkanne

watering can

Sense

scythe

Pflug

plough

Sichel

sickle

Hacke

hoe

Mistgabel

pitchfork

Axt

axe

Schubkarre

wheelbarrow

Trog

trough

Milchkanne

milk can

Sack

sack

Zaun

fence

Stall

stable

Treibhaus

greenhouse

Boden

soil

Saat

seed

Dünger

fertilizer

Mähdrescher

combine harvester

ernten

harvest

Ernte

harvest

Yamswurzel

yams

Weizen

wheat

Soja

soy

Erdapfel

potato

Mais

corn

Raps

rapeseed

Obstbaum

fruit tree

Maniok

cassava

Getreide

cereals

Schornstein
chimney

Dach
roof

Regenrinne
drainpipe

Fenster
window

Garage
garage

Klingel
doorbell

Tür
door

Abfallkübel
rubbish bin

Briefkasten
letterbox

Garten
garden

Wohnzimmer

living room

Badezimmer

bathroom

Küche

kitchen

Schlafzimmer

bedroom

Kinderzimmer

child's room

Esszimmer

dining room

Boden

floor

Wand

wall

Decke

ceiling

Keller

cellar

Sauna

sauna

Balkon

balcony

Terrasse

terrace

Schwimmbad

pool

Rasenmäher

lawn mower

Bettbezug

sheet

Bettdecke

bedspread

Bett

bed

Besen

broom

Kübel

bucket

Schalter

switch

Haus - house

Tapete
wallpaper

Bild
picture

Lampe
lamp

Regal
shelf

Schrank
cupboard

Kamin
fireplace

Fernseher
television

Blume
flower

Polster
cushion

Vase
vase

Sofa
sofa

Fernbedienung
remote control

Teppich

carpet

Vorhang

curtain

Tisch

table

Sessel

chair

Schaukelstuhl

rocking chair

Sessel

armchair

Buch

book

Decke

blanket

Dekoration

decoration

Feuerholz

firewood

Film

film

Stereoanlage

hi-fi equipment

Schlüssel

key

Zeitung

newspaper

Gemälde

painting

Poster

poster

Radio

radio

Notizblock

notepad

Staubsauger

hoover

Kaktus

cactus

Kerze

candle

Kühlschrank
fridge

Mikrowelle
microwave oven

Küchenwaage
kitchen scales

Toaster
toaster

Reinigungsmittel
detergent

Backofen
oven

Gefrierfach
freezer

Abfallkübel
rubbish bin

Geschirrspüler
dishwasher

Herd

cooker

Topf

pot

Eisentopf

cast-iron pot

Wok / Kadai

wok / kadai

Pfanne

pan

Wasserkocher

kettle

Dampfgarer

steamer

Backblech

baking tray

Geschirr

crockery

Becher

mug

Schale

bowl

Essstäbchen

chopsticks

Schöpflöffel

ladle

Pfannenwender

spatula

Schneebesen

whisk

Kochsieb

strainer

Sieb

sieve

Reibe

grater

Mörser

mortar

Grill

barbecue

Kaminfeuer

open fire

Küche - kitchen

Schneidebrett

chopping board

Nudelholz

rolling pin

Korkenzieher

corkscrew

Dose

can

Dosenöffner

can opener

Topflappen

pot holder

Waschbecken

sink

Bürste

brush

Schwamm

sponge

Mixer

blender

Gefriertruhe

deep freezer

Babyflasche

baby bottle

Wasserhahn

tap

Badezimmer
bathroom

Heizung
heating

Dusche
shower

Handtuch
towel

Duschvorhang
shower curtain

Schaumbad
bubble bath

Badewanne
bathtub

Glas
glass

Waschmaschine
washing machine

Wasserhahn
tap

Fliesen
tiles

Nachttopf
potty

Waschbecken
sink

Klo
toilet

Hocktoilette
squat toilet

Bidet
bidet

Pissoir
urinal

Klopapier
toilet paper

Klobürste
toilet brush

Zahnbürste

toothbrush

Zahnpasta

toothpaste

Zahnseide

dental floss

waschen

wash

Handbrause

handheld shower

Intimdusche

douche

Waschschüssel

basin

Rückenbürste

back brush

Seife

soap

Duschgel

shower gel

Shampoo

shampoo

Waschlappen

flannel

Abfluss

drain

Creme

cream

Deodorant

deodorant

Badezimmer - bathroom

Spiegel

mirror

Kosmetikspiegel

hand mirror

Rasierer

razor

Rasierschaum

shaving foam

Rasierwasser

aftershave

Kamm

comb

Bürste

brush

Föhn

hair dryer

Haarspray

hairspray

Makeup

makeup

Lippenstift

lipstick

Nagellack

nail varnish

Watte

cotton wool

Nagelschere

nail scissors

Parfum

perfume

Kulturbeutel

washbag

Hocker

stool

Waage

weighing scale

Bademantel

bathrobe

Gummihandschuhe

rubber gloves

Tampon

tampon

Damenbinde

sanitary towel

Chemietoilette

chemical toilet

Kinderzimmer
child's room

Wecker
alarm clock

Kuscheltier
cuddly toy

Spielzeugauto
toy car

Rassel
rattle

Puppenhaus
doll's house

Geschenk
present

Ballon

balloon

Bett

bed

Kinderwagen

pram

Kartenspiel

deck of cards

Puzzle

jigsaw

Comic

comic

Legosteine

lego bricks

Bausteine

building blocks

Actionfigur

action figure

Strampelanzug

babygrow

Frisbee

frisbee

Mobile

mobile

Brettspiel

board game

Würfel

dice

Modelleisenbahn

model train set

Schnuller

dummy

Party

party

Bilderbuch

picture book

Ball

ball

Puppe

doll

spielen

play

Sandkasten

sandpit

Schaukel

swing

Spielzeug

toys

Spielkonsole

video game console

Dreirad

tricycle

Teddy

teddy bear

Kleiderschrank

wardrobe

Kleidung
clothing

Socken

socks

Strümpfe

stockings

Strumpfhose

tights

Schal
scarf

Gürtel
belt

Regenschirm
umbrella

T-Shirt
t-shirt

Turnschuhe
trainers

Stiefel
boots

Hausschuhe
slippers

Sandalen

sandals

Schuhe

shoes

Gummistiefel

rubber boots

Unterhose

underpants

Büstenhalter

bra

Unterhemd

vest

Kleidung - clothing

45

Body

body

Hose

trousers

Jeans

jeans

Rock

skirt

Bluse

blouse

Hemd

shirt

Pullover

pullover

Kapuzenpullover

hoodie

Blazer

blazer

Jacke

jacket

Mantel

coat

Regenmantel

raincoat

Kostüm

costume

Kleid

dress

Hochzeitskleid

wedding dress

Anzug

suit

Nachthemd

nightgown

Pyjama

pyjamas

Sari

sari

Kopftuch

headscarf

Turban

turban

Burka

burqa

Kaftan

kaftan

Abaya

abaya

Badeanzug

swimsuit

Badehose

trunks

kurze Hose

shorts

Jogginganzug

tracksuit

Schürze

apron

Handschuhe

gloves

Knopf

button

Brille

glasses

Armband

bracelet

Halskette

necklace

Ring

ring

Ohrring

earring

Mütze

cap

Kleiderbügel

coat hanger

Hut

hat

Krawatte

tie

Reißverschluss

zip

Helm

helmet

Hosenträger

braces

Schuluniform

school uniform

Uniform

uniform

Lätzchen

bib

Schnuller

dummy

Windel

nappy

Server
server

Aktenschrank
filing cabinet

Drucker
printer

Monitor
monitor

Papier
paper

Maus
mouse

Schreibtisch
desk

Ordner
folder

Tastatur
keyboard

Papierkorb
waste-paper basket

Computer
computer

Sessel
chair

Kaffeebecher

coffee mug

Taschenrechner

calculator

Internet

internet

Laptop

laptop

Brief

letter

Nachricht

message

Handy

mobile

Netzwerk

network

Kopierer

photocopier

Software

software

Telefon

telephone

Steckdose

plug socket

Fax

fax machine

Formular

form

Dokument

document

kaufen
buy

bezahlen
pay

handeln
trade

Geld
money

Dollar
dollar

Euro
euro

Yen
yen

Rubel
rouble

Franken
Swiss franc

Renminbi Yuan
renminbi yuan

Rupie
rupee

Bankomat
cashpoint

Wechselstube

bureau de change

Gold

gold

Silber

silver

Öl

oil

Energie

energy

Preis

price

Vertrag

contract

Steuer

tax

Aktie

stock

arbeiten

work

Angestellte

employee

Arbeitgeber

employer

Fabrik

factory

Geschäft

shop

Wirtschaft - economy

Polizist
police officer

Feuerwehrmann
fireman

Koch
cook

Ärztin
doctor

Pilot
pilot

Gärtner

gardener

Tischler

carpenter

Schneiderin

seamstress

Richter

judge

Chemikerin

chemist

Schauspieler

actor

Busfahrer

bus driver

Taxifahrer

taxi driver

Fischer

fisherman

Putzfrau

cleaning lady

Dachdecker

roofer

Kellner

waiter

Jäger

hunter

Maler

painter

Bäcker

baker

Elektriker

electrician

Bauarbeiter

builder

Ingenieur

engineer

Schlachter

butcher

Installateur

plumber

Briefträgerin

postman

Soldat

soldier

Architekt

architect

Kassiererin

cashier

Blumenhändlerin

florist

Friseur

hairdresser

Schaffner

conductor

Mechaniker

mechanic

Kapitän

captain

Zahnärztin

dentist

Wissenschaftler

scientist

Rabbi

rabbi

Imam

imam

Mönch

monk

Pfarrer

clergyman

Hammer
hammer

Zange
pliers

Schraubenzieher
screwdriver

Schraubenschlüssel
spanner

Taschenlampe
torch

Bagger

digger

Werkzeugkasten

toolbox

Leiter

ladder

Säge

saw

Nägel

nails

Bohrer

drill

reparieren

repair

Schaufel

shovel

Scheiße!

Damn!

Kehrschaufel

dustpan

Farbtopf

paint pot

Schrauben

screws

Musikinstrumente
musical instruments

Schlagzeug
drum kit

Lautsprecher
loudspeaker

Gitarre
guitar

Kontrabass
double bass

Trompete
trumpet

Klavier

piano

Violine

violin

Bass

bass

Pauke

timpani

Trommeln

drums

Tastatur

keyboard

Saxophon

saxophone

Flöte

flute

Mikrofon

microphone

Eingang
entrance

Tiger
tiger

Käfig
cage

Zebra
zebra

Tierfutter
animal feed

Panda
panda

Tiere

animals

Elefant

elephant

Känguru

kangaroo

Nashorn

rhino

Gorilla

gorilla

Bär

bear

Kamel

camel

Strauß

ostrich

Löwe

lion

Affe

monkey

Flamingo

flamingo

Papagei

parrot

Eisbär

polar bear

Pinguin

penguin

Hai

shark

Pfau

peacock

Schlange

snake

Krokodil

crocodile

Zoowärter

zookeeper

Robbe

seal

Jaguar

jaguar

Pony

pony

Leopard

leopard

Nilpferd

hippo

Giraffe

giraffe

Adler

eagle

Wildschwein

boar

Fisch

fish

Schildkröte

turtle

Walross

walrus

Fuchs

fox

Gazelle

gazelle

Zoo - zoo

American Football
American football

Radfahren
cycling

Tennis
tennis

Basketball
basketball

Schwimmen
swimming

Boxen
boxing

Eishockey
ice hockey

Fußball
football

Badminton
badminton

Leichtathletik
athletics

Handball
handball

Skifahren
skiing

Polo
polo

springen
jump

lachen
laugh

umarmen
hug

gehen
walk

singen
sing

träumen
dream

beten
pray

küssen
kiss

schreiben

write

zeichnen

draw

zeigen

show

drücken

push

geben

give

nehmen

take

haben

have

machen

do

sein

be

stehen

stand

laufen

run

ziehen

pull

werfen

throw

fallen

fall

liegen

lie

warten

wait

tragen

carry

sitzen

sit

anziehen

get dressed

schlafen

sleep

aufwachen

wake up

ansehen

look at

weinen

cry

streicheln

stroke

frisieren

comb

reden

talk

verstehen

understand

fragen

ask

hören

listen

trinken

drink

essen

eat

zusammenräumen

tidy up

lieben

love

kochen

cook

fahren

drive

fliegen

fly

Aktivitäten - activities

segeln

sail

rechnen

calculate

lesen

read

lernen

learn

arbeiten

work

heiraten

marry

nähen

sew

Zähne putzen

brush teeth

töten

kill

rauchen

smoke

senden

send

Aktivitäten - activities

Großmutter
grandmother

Großvater
grandfather

Vater
father

Mutter
mother

Baby
baby

Tochter
daughter

Sohn
son

Gast
guest

Tante
aunt

Onkel
uncle

Bruder
brother

Schwester
sister

Stirn
forehead

Auge
eye

Schulter
shoulder

Gesicht
face

Finger
finger

Kinn
chin

Hand
hand

Brust
breast

Bein
leg

Arm
arm

Baby

baby

Mann

man

Frau

woman

Mädchen

girl

Junge

boy

Kopf

head

Rücken

back

Bauch

belly

Nabel

belly button

Zeh

toe

Ferse

heel

Knochen

bone

Hüfte

hip

Knie

knee

Ellbogen

elbow

Nase

nose

Gesäß

bottom

Haut

skin

Wange

cheek

Ohr

ear

Lippe

lip

Körper - body

69

Mund

mouth

Zahn

tooth

Zunge

tongue

Gehirn

brain

Herz

heart

Muskel

muscle

Lunge

lung

Leber

liver

Magen

stomach

Nieren

kidneys

Geschlechtsverkehr

sex

Kondom

condom

Eizelle

ovum

Sperma

semen

Schwangerschaft

pregnancy

Körper - body

Menstruation

menstruation

Vagina

vagina

Penis

penis

Augenbraue

eyebrow

Haar

hair

Hals

neck

Spital
hospital

Rettung
ambulance

Rollstuhl
wheelchair

Bruch
fracture

Ärztin

doctor

Notaufnahme

emergency room

Krankenschwester

nurse

Notfall

emergency

ohnmächtig

unconscious

Schmerz

pain

Verletzung

injury

Blutung

bleeding

Herzinfarkt

heart attack

Schlaganfall

stroke

Allergie

allergy

Husten

cough

Fieber

fever

Grippe

flu

Durchfall

diarrhoea

Kopfschmerzen

headache

Krebs

cancer

Diabetes

diabetes

Chirurg

surgeon

Skalpell

scalpel

Operation

operation

CT

CT

Röntgen

x-ray

Ultraschall

ultrasound

Maske

face mask

Krankheit

disease

Wartezimmer

waiting room

Krücke

crutch

Pflaster

plaster

Verband

bandage

Injektion

injection

Stethoskop

stethoscope

Trage

stretcher

Thermometer

clinical thermometer

Geburt

birth

Übergewicht

overweight

Hörgerät

hearing aid

Desinfektionsmittel

disinfectant

Infektion

infection

Virus

virus

HIV / AIDS

HIV / AIDS

Medizin

medicine

Impfung

vaccination

Tabletten

tablets

Pille

pill

Notruf

emergency call

Blutdruckmesser

blood pressure monitor

krank / gesund

ill / healthy

Hilfe!

Help!

Alarm

alarm

Überfall

assault

Angriff

attack

Gefahr

danger

Notausgang

emergency exit

Feuer!

Fire!

Feuerlöscher

fire extinguisher

Unfall

accident

Erste-Hilfe-Koffer

first-aid kit

SOS

SOS

Polizei

police

Europa

Europe

Nordamerika

North America

Südamerika

South America

Afrika

Africa

Asien

Asia

Australien

Australia

Atlantik

Atlantic

Pazifik

Pacific

Indische Ozean

Indian Ocean

Antarktische Ozean

Antarctic Ocean

Arktische Ozean

Arctic Ocean

Nordpol

North Pole

Südpol

South Pole

Antarktis

Antarctica

Erde

Earth

Land

land

Meer

sea

Insel

island

Nation

nation

Staat

state

Ziffernblatt

clock face

Stundenzeiger

hour hand

Minutenzeiger

minute hand

Sekundenzeiger

second hand

Wie spät ist es?

What time is it?

Tag

day

Zeit

time

jetzt

now

Digitaluhr

digital watch

Minute

minute

Stunde

hour

Woche
week

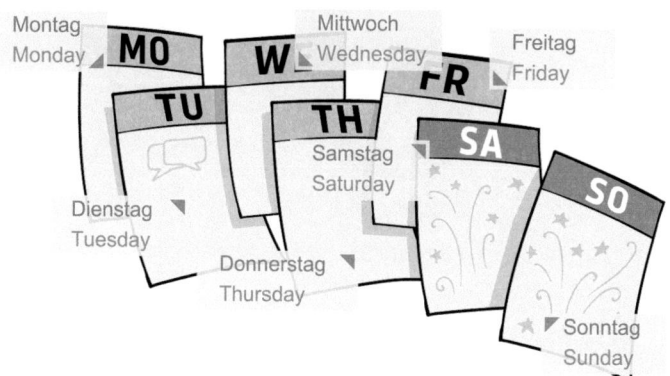

Montag / Monday — MO
Dienstag / Tuesday — TU
Mittwoch / Wednesday — WE
Donnerstag / Thursday — TH
Freitag / Friday — FR
Samstag / Saturday — SA
Sonntag / Sunday — SO

gestern

yesterday

heute

today

morgen

tomorrow

Morgen

morning

Mittag

noon

Abend

evening

MO	TU	WE	TH	FR	SA	SU
1	2	3	4	5	6	7
8	9	10	11	12	13	14
15	16	17	18	19	20	21
22	23	24	25	26	27	28
29	30	31	1	2	3	4

Arbeitstage

business days

MO	TU	WE	TH	FR	SA	SU
1	2	3	4	5	6	7
8	9	10	11	12	13	14
15	16	17	18	19	20	21
22	23	24	25	26	27	28
29	30	31	1	2	3	4

Wochenende

weekend

Regen
rain

Regenbogen
rainbow

Schnee
snow

Wind
wind

Frühling
spring

Herbst
autumn

Sommer
summer

Winter
winter

Wettervorhersage

weather forecast

Thermometer

thermometer

Sonnenschein

sunshine

Wolke

cloud

Nebel

fog

Luftfeuchtigkeit

humidity

Blitz

lightning

Donner

thunder

Sturm

storm

Hagel

hail

Monsun

monsoon

Flut

flood

Eis

ice

Jänner

January

Februar

February

März

March

April

April

Mai

May

Juni

June

Juli

July

August

August

Jahr - year

September
....
September

Oktober
....
October

November
....
November

Dezember
....
December

Kreis
....
circle

Quadrat
....
square

Rechteck
....
rectangle

Dreieck
....
triangle

Kugel
....
sphere

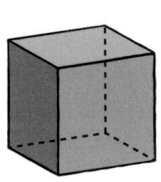

Würfel
....
cube

Farben
colours

weiß

white

gelb

yellow

orange

orange

pink

pink

rot

red

lila

purple

blau

blue

grün

green

braun

brown

grau

grey

schwarz

black

viel / wenig

a lot / a little

wütend / friedlich

angry / calm

hübsch / hässlich

beautiful / ugly

Anfang / Ende

beginning / end

groß / klein

big / small

hell / dunkel

bright / dark

Bruder / Schwester

brother / sister

sauber / schmutzig

clean / dirty

vollständig / unvollständig

complete / incomplete

Tag / Nacht

day / night

tot / lebendig

dead / alive

breit / schmal

wide / narrow

genießbar / ungenießbar

edible / inedible

böse / freundlich

evil / kind

aufgeregt / gelangweilt

excited / bored

dick / dünn

fat / thin

zuerst / zuletzt

first / last

Freund / Feind

friend / enemy

voll / leer

full / empty

hart / weich

hard / soft

schwer / leicht

heavy / light

Hunger / Durst

hunger / thirst

krank / gesund

ill / healthy

illegal / legal

illegal / legal

gescheit / dumm

intelligent / stupid

links / rechts

left / right

nah / fern

near / far

neu / gebraucht

new / used

nichts / etwas

nothing / something

alt / jung

old / young

an / aus

on / off

offen / geschlossen

open / closed

leise / laut

quiet / loud

reich / arm

rich / poor

richtig / falsch

right / wrong

rau / glatt

rough / smooth

traurig / glücklich

sad / happy

kurz / lang

short / long

langsam / schnell

slow / fast

nass / trocken

wet / dry

warm / kühl

warm / cool

Krieg / Frieden

war / peace

0	**1**	**2**
null	eins	zwei
zero	one	two
3	**4**	**5**
drei	vier	fünf
three	four	five
6	**7**	**8**
sechs	sieben	acht
six	seven	eight
9	**10**	**11**
neun	zehn	elf
nine	ten	eleven

12

zwölf

twelve

13

dreizehn

thirteen

14

vierzehn

fourteen

15

fünfzehn

fifteen

16

sechzehn

sixteen

17

siebzehn

seventeen

18

achtzehn

eighteen

19

neunzehn

nineteen

20

zwanzig

twenty

100

hundert

hundred

1.000

tausend

thousand

1.000.000

Million

million

Englisch

English

Amerikanisches Englisch

American English

Chinesisch (Mandarin)

Chinese Mandarin

Hindi

Hindi

Spanisch

Spanish

Französisch

French

Arabisch

Arabic

Russisch

Russian

Portugiesisch

Portuguese

Bengalisch

Bengali

Deutsch

German

Japanisch

Japanese

ich

I

du

you

er / sie / es

he / she / it

wir

we

ihr

you

sie

they

Wer?

who?

Was?

what?

Wie?

how?

Wo?

where?

Wann?

when?

Name

name

hinter

behind

in

in

vor

in front of

über

over

auf

on

unter

under

neben

beside

zwischen

between

Ort

place